Hells Canyon
America's Deepest Gorge

The Inside Story of an Impossible Victory

By

Larry Williams, Brock Evans and Doug Scott

Pete Seeger is floating through Hells Canyon flying his homemade "Save Hells Canyon" flag. Boyd Norton at the oars, July 1972.

Intentionally Left Blank

Contents

ACKNOWLEDGMENTS

We could not have produced this manuscript without the invaluable aid of several historians whose suggestions we incorporated. Thanks to Ronald Eber, historian for the Oregon Chapter of the Sierra Club, past Chair and Wilderness Coordinator from 1980-1985 and Gerald Williams, retired historian in the office of the Chief of the Forest Service. We adopted their every suggestion--and appreciate the editing assistance of Dr. Lynne Corn, former Specialist in Natural Resources at the Congressional Research Service. Our thanks to Rodney Stubbs, founding board member of the Oregon Environmental Council (OEC) for publishing this story and our photo editor Tom Sliter.

A number of the volunteer leaders assisted with a close reading and materials in their files and their memories—our purpose here has been to capture those as part of the unreported inside story. Thanks to the Greater Hells Canyon Council leaders Pete Henault, Jerry Jayne, Boyd Norton, Jim Campbell, Dale Storey, John Barker, and Pete Sandrock. Photographs were taken by Larry Williams.

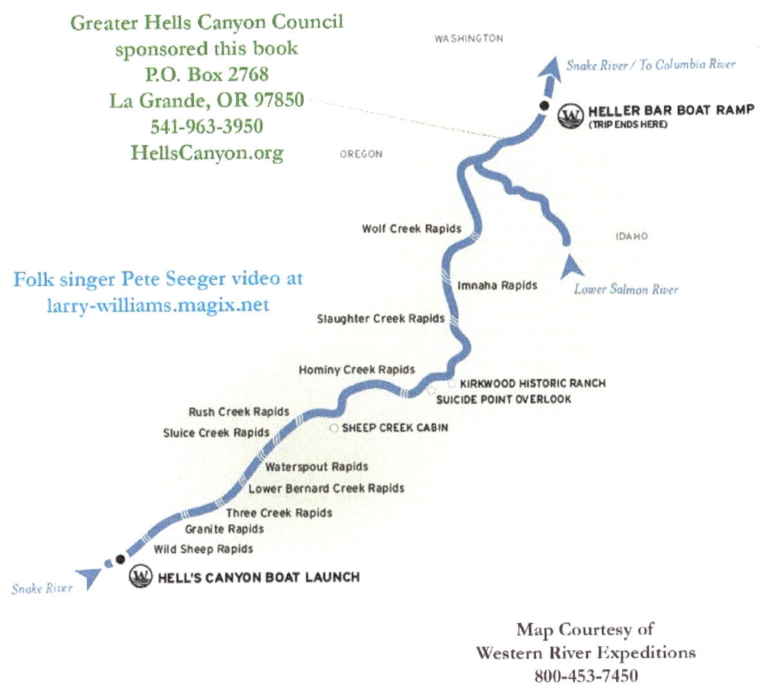

Map Courtesy of
Western River Expeditions
800-453-7450

INTRODUCTION

On July 31, 1976 conservation history was made where the fast-flowing Snake River in Hells Canyon forms the border between Oregon and Idaho. Here a ceremony was held on the Oregon rim to dedicate the new Hells Canyon National Recreation Area. This dedication prohibited any future dams in the canyon and designated the Middle Snake Wild River and Hells Canyon Wilderness Area.[1] This is the story of how this dedication came to be.

A Perfect Dam Site

The great Washington state outdoorsman, U.S. Supreme Court Justice, William O. Douglas gives the big picture.

"These waterways flow out of the most deeply scarred and rugged canyons on the continent. It is 7900 feet from the lip of the ridge to the surface of the water." "Here the Astor overland party foundered. Here Captain Benjamin L. E. Bonneville was turned back. Here the Snake is one of the most treacherous of all rivers to run."2

The fast-flowing Snake River forms the border between Oregon and Idaho. The canyon is a perfect site for a hydroelectric dam, but it also produces nearly 40 percent of all salmon and steelhead in the Columbia River Basin. It carries nearly twice the water volume of the Colorado River. It's of little wonder that this wild place was named Hells Canyon. The first reference to the name Hells Canyon appears in an 1895 edition of *McCurdy's Marine History of the Pacific Northwest.*³ This remote place became the center of a power struggle between dam builders and wilderness advocates in the 1960's that would change the politics of the Pacific Northwest.

This is the rest of the story, told by those who were closely involved in the many twists and turns leading ultimately to the protection of the magnificent river from dams that would have destroyed its wild character and valuable native salmon runs.

First Impressions –

Its Hills are Mountains High. In June of 1806, as The Corps of Discovery returned from the Pacific seeking an easier passage across the Rocky Mountains, Captain Meriwether Lewis wrote in his journal: "About Noon Sergt. Ordway Frazier and Wizer returned with 17 salmon and some roots of the cows; the distance was so great from which they had brought the fish that most of them were nearly spoiled, there fish were as fat as any I ever saw; sufficiently so to cook themselves without the addition of grease; those which were sound were extremely delicious; their flesh is of a fine rose colour with a small admixture of yellow."

The journal report continues, "the balance of their route was through a high broken mountainous country generally well timbered with pine in this quarter the soil fertility they met with an abundance of deer and some big horned animals."

The East Fork of "Lewis's River" they describe as:

"One continued rapid about 150 yds. wide it's banks are in most places solid and perpendicular rocks, which rise to a great height. On the tops of some of those hills over which they passed the snow had not entirely disappeared, and the grass was just springing up at the fishery on Lewis's river below the forks there is a very considerable rapid nearly as great from the information of Sergt Ordway as the great falls of the Columbia rapids the river 200 Yds. wide."

Thus, the canyon previously known only to Indians and those "big horned animals" first entered the history books. In the 1830's, U.S. Army Captain Bonneville wrote of his first encounter with the spectacular Canyon,

"Nothing we had ever gazed upon in any other region could for a moment compare in wild majesty and impressive sternness with the series of scenes which here at every turn astonished our senses and filled us with awe and delight."

Years after early explorers dismissed the area placer miners discovered gold in 1860, but not in Hells Canyon itself. Hardrock miners had more success, leading to operations that helped create and support some of the communities in the area, most of which are ghost towns today. In the late 1800's homesteaders began arriving in the area hoping to raise cattle and sheep and their families. The gentle slopes surrounding Hells Canyon offered a good living. However, the harsh winters discouraged many. Abandoned farm implements keep alive of the memory of their presence. In the 1830's, U.S. Army Captain Bonneville wrote of his first encounter with the spectacular Canyon,

"Nothing we had ever gazed upon in any other region could for a moment compare in wild majesty and impressive sternness with the series of scenes which here at every turn astonished our senses and filled us with awe and delight."

In the next century, those few who knew the Middle Snake considered it impassable, certainly not boat-able, and far too remote for tourism. But there were others who lusted to control and wanted to harness the river's power with a mega dam—a so-called "High Dam."

DAM-BUILDERS FOCUS ON HELLS CANYON

Hells Canyon was always viewed as remote, inhospitable and a great place for a dam. Well-known Oregon writer and future Senator Richard L. Neuberger (D-OR) described the immensity of Hells Canyon and its potential for a hydropower dam:

"No highway or railroad can get into it. Trails hewn out of granite and basalt by CCC works are the sole venue of the entrance. The hands and foreheads of airplane pilots are clammy as they fly over this forbidding area. Engine trouble or a broken strut in the air means death below. There is not an acre of level ground in the ominous hinterland that the Seven Devils [Mountains, in Idaho] guard. Through one of the gorges that split the range the Snake River rushes. From Devil Peak to the silvery strip of water in Hells Canyon way beneath, the drop is a sheer seventy-nine hundred feet. It is more than two thousand feet deeper than the Grand Canyon of Colorado River. For grandeur and breathtaking immensity, there is no sight in the country to compare with the cleft the Snake has dug along the Oregon-Idaho boundary, a gorge that is relatively unknown and rarely visited only because it is so inaccessible. ... Even hardened forest rangers come away from it with frail and wobbly knees."

At this stage of his life and writing, Neuberger only saw the river rushing through this gorge in terms of what man could do with it with enough dollars and enough daring: "The flats and tablelands are dry and arid now, but they could be checkered with farms and orchards." How?

"The water that has cut Hells Canyon seventy-nine hundred feet into the earth's surface can also make the sagebrush regions bloom. Water! That is the magician's fluid to transform the blank spaces

on the census map into mottled areas representing thickly clustered farms and thriving towns. Irrigation is the artery of life to thousands of Western farms."[4]

Neuberger knew what was needed to drive this great path to progress: electricity:

"Where the roaring Snake joins [the Columbia] after a rush through the deepest gorge of the hemisphere, the river snarls like an angry monster. Over falls and cascades it booms the mightiest power anthem in North America. Wild and defiant, the river tumbles unharnessed to the Pacific."

Neuberger had the bug—and he had it bad. He put it all together for his New Deal enthusiast readers:

"For years every business man and banker and industrialist in the Far West has dreamed this dream. From the time the corps of army engineers first reported that the Columbia River watershed contained almost as much potential power as all the other rivers of the nation combined, storekeepers in Oregon and manufacturers in Washington have envisioned an array of Pittsburgh's in the Northwest. Are not all the necessary ingredients available —deep harbors, thick stand of timber, untapped pockets of minerals, mild climate, fertile soil, ample rainfall, unlimited hydroelectricity?"[5]

The future Oregon Senator Neuberger had experienced a mental, emotional, and ultimately political transformation.

Powerful economic interests in the 1930's began a campaign to dam all the Northwest's great rivers, beginning with the Columbia. Rock Island dam was the first across the main stem in central Washington. It was completed in 1933. Four New Deal-era federal dams followed—Bonneville (1938), Grand Coulee (1941), McNary (1953), and Chief Joseph (1955), with more planned.

In 1947, the Federal Power Commission (FPC) licensed

the Idaho Power Company to build a three-dam complex in uppermost Hells Canyon. This led to Brownlee Dam, completed in 1959, followed by Oxbow in 1960. Above the Middle Snake reach, Hells Canyon Dam—later termed the "Low Dam"—was completed in 1967, the first dam in the canyon.

1 Hells Canyon Dam at the upstream access to the Gorge

The plan was to continue by damming the Snake River below the Hells Canyon Dam.

On Memorial Day 1948, Vanport, Oregon, a Portland suburb, was devastated by a flood.[6] Responding to public opinion, President Harry Truman championed a Hells Canyon High Dam as part of an all-out effort for flood control and a demonstration of continuing support for President Franklin D. Roosevelt's New Deal. Truman's 1949 budget proposed billions for new dams, including this one.[7] But conservative Idaho agricultural interests blocked these plans. Then the new President Dwight Eisenhower lent his support for the High Dam, but one built by private interests, not the federal government.[8] This was to be a model for his policy of "partnership." When he became president, prospects for building a privately funded dam in Hells Canyon looked bright.

2 Campsite in the deepest gorge in America

Nothing happened until 1963 when the Forest Service approved a new scenic area—the 130,000-acre Hells Canyon-Seven Devils Scenic Area.

The scenic area encompassed parts of the Wallowa-Whitman National forest in Oregon and the Nez Perce and Payette National forests in Idaho. The area extended for some 22 miles along the Snake River north of Homestead, Oregon. Unfortunately, it did not deter the FPC.

The Commission ruled on February 5, 1964 by a vote of 3 to 2, for the Pacific Northwest Power Company's (PNPC) High Mountain Sheep Dam. It was deemed most suitable to provide:

"The best comprehensive development which would avoid fish passage problems to the Salmon River."

On March 9, 1964, the FPC granted a license to build the High Mountain Sheep Dam to PNPC.

The Washington Public Power Supply System went to federal court arguing that approval of a privately built dam was against the public interest because it violated the public/private power clause of the Federal Power Act. By 1967, the case was awaiting a Supreme Court decision. The only issue before the court was the question of "who"— which power combine, public or private power—would get the license. Not "whether"--just who. Protecting Hells Canyon from the dam builders appeared to be an impossible cause. Nevertheless, leaders of the Pacific Northwest Chapter of the Sierra Club at their spring 1967 meeting directed their newly appointed northwest representative, Seattle attorney Brock Evans, to do what he could to save the canyon from the dam.

"If ever there was a hopeless cause, it was stopping any new dams in Hells Canyon," Evans recalled. "The Supreme Court was already addressing the only issue: who would get to build it?"

Evans began by helping to organize local groups in Idaho and Oregon.

On June 5, 1967, the high court surprised everyone, remanding the High Mountain Sheep case back to the Federal

Power Commission with instructions to consider another option. Writing for the majority, Justice William O. Douglas, a north westerner and outdoorsman who had hiked the canyon 17 years earlier, ruled:

"The question here is not who will build the dam—but rather whether it is in public interest to build any dam at all…or, should the wild river wilderness be preserved…."

He further commented, "That determination can be made only after all issues were considered, the court ruled, including the public interest in preserving reaches of wild rivers and wilderness areas, the preservation of anadromous fish for commercial and recreational purposes, and the protection of wildlife."[10]

3 The water volume of the Snake River is twice the size of the Colorado River

The Congress had already recognized the importance of preserving such supremely wild places as wilderness areas and protecting America's free-flowing rivers with the passage of the Wilderness Act of 1964, and (after the FPC decision) the Wild and Scenic Rivers Act of 1968. These new laws and a long history of preserving national parks continued to inspire conservationists. Justice William O. Douglas wrote:

"Raw wilderness is perhaps one of the most arresting features of the State [of Idaho]. The Hell's [sic] Canyon passage of the Snake River is one of the great American wilderness regions. For those willing to exchange flat pavement for terrain that virtually stands on end, a trip through the Snake River Gorge is an unforgettable experience."[11]

With this decision, Evans saw a new path to defeat the dam. He spent much of the next six weeks researching and preparing a Petition of Intervention[12] asking the FPC to admit conservationists as full parties in the new FPC proceeding in order to argue in defense of the public interest in a free-flowing wild river.[13] This Petition was filed in the name of the Sierra Club, Federation of Western Outdoor Clubs, and Idaho Alpine Club. He mailed the Petition and 20 copies thereof, around midnight August 31 meeting the September 1 deadline.[14] The Petition was granted on September 25, 1967, marking the first time a case to preserve wilderness would be presented in a court. It was a daunting challenge. As Senator Neuberger had long argued, the FPC was *"an agency to license concrete-pouring."*[15]

Evans asked Tom Brucker, a friend and more experienced attorney, to be co-counsel opposing the dam and defending the wild river. The case would be called "High Mountain Sheep." The two began a three-year intense routine of retiring to Brucker's home with volumes of law books and witness testimonies before each major hearing.

"Oh, what a howl from attorneys for the dam builders, both public and private power, when we intervened," Evans recalled. "Although they were most unhappy about Justice William O. Douglas's opinion and the subsequent remand for a new trial, they were confident that they had worked out a cozy little deal with the

FPC trial judge. The hearing examiner, the Honorable William Levy, was pro-dam and determined to get the trial 'over with' and issue a new license. That's when both entities, private and public, started working together."[16]

A pre-trial conference was held on September 28, 1967 in Portland:

"the date is still burned into my brain," remembers Evans, "for the 30 attorneys representing the three states, the Farm Bureau Federation, native Indian tribes, unions and business groups, I began to understand just how great were the forces aligned against us—all the fat cat attorneys and all their Big Money posturing … and we, little 'us,' at the very end—daring to speak out for a wild river![17] *"In October and November" Evans recalls "we gained important new allies. Thirty groups, local, regional and national flocked to the support the new cause – No More Dams' and building new hope and momentum among conservationists."*

The more experienced "Brucker coolly made our case."[18] We tried it together over the next three years. In 1971, Levy again issued a license for the dam—but, noting the extensive factual evidence presented about wild rivers as well as the passion and expertise of the pro-river witnesses, he granted a three-year moratorium, in which time period the groups can seek legislation from Congress.[19]

Representative Al Ullman (D-OR), whose district included the Oregon side of the canyon river, also was not happy about the new delay; he saw an FPC license "as the only practical way we can get this river developed."[20]

THE LEGISLATIVE DANCE BEGINS

At first, the grassroots interest in protection came from a group of engineers at the National Reactor Testing Station near Idaho Falls who regularly floated the river. However, the scenic area approved by the Forest Service in 1963 for the 130,000-acre Hells Canyon-Seven Devils Scenic Area did not prohibit the proposals for dams.[21]

4 Time to take in the beauty of the Snake River on the Oregon/Idaho border

In March, 1967, Russ Mager, an invited speaker, showed his slides of the canyon to the Idaho Alpine Club. In response to the threats a small group met in Russ Mager's living room that summer in Pocatello and formed the Hells Canyon Preservation Council (HCPC).[22] Russ Mager became their first president.

"We were new at this sort of thing," said another engineer Jerry Jayne, "we were feeling our way and trying to get organized and set up a formal organization to oppose a dam. "[23]

Before the FPC could rule, Evans and Clif Merritt, western field representative for The Wilderness Society, had gathered with the new HCPC leaders on September 9–10, 1967, at boatman Floyd Harvey's Willow Bar Camp in Hells Canyon for their first strategy session. They concluded that a national park was not feasible because national parks prohibit hunting. Powerful sport hunting organizations would mount intense opposition. They settled on something new: a Hells Canyon-Snake National River.[24] The strategy was to gain delay and generate as much publicity as possible to try to move elected officials away from their support for the dam. This was no small task so the conservationists needed to muster grassroots and media support.

"Remember Justice Douglas's decision again, ordering that the FPC must first ask … whether the project will be in the public interest,'" Evans says. "This single word "whether" was how this obiter dictum opinion came to save the day. It gave us a unique, precious opening and, because the Supreme Court decreed it, it is the law. Evans drafted a bill in early 1968 in consultation with Clif Merritt and the HCPC leaders. Finding a Congressional sponsor was another matter. "We tried to shop our draft bill around the Congress without much luck."[25]

5 (L to R) Larry Williams, Oregon Environmental Council, Joe Walicki, The Wilderness Society; and Brock Evans, The Sierra Club, testifying before the Senate Environment and Public Works Committee.

FINDING CONGRESSIONAL SUPPORT

In the eight years prior to the court decision, however, Senator Frank Church (D-ID), a good conservationist with many sportsman friends, had begun to reconsider his earlier position supporting dams.[26] However, because the proposed Nez Perce Dam (later replaced by the application for the proposed High Mountain Sheep site) threatened to block Idaho's famous River of No Return, Church was opposed.

The Salmon River was home to 30 percent of the total anadromous fish spawning in the Columbia Basin and more than half of all its spring and summer Chinook salmon. In 1959 and again in October 1968 Church and Senator Leonard Jordan (R-ID), introduced a moratorium bill, prohibiting any new dams in Hells Canyon until 1978. The bill (S. 3320), reintroduced in the next Congress, passed the Senate in late 1969.

If the bill became law it would buy time for preservationists to build a case to ban all dams in Hells Canyon. In a "Dear Friend" letter to Senate colleagues, Church stated:

> *"if preservation of the river in its natural state is the highest use— and I incline to that view—the moratorium should buy the required time to prove the case."*[27]

On November 8, 1968 conservationists released a press release:

> ***"New National Area Proposed for Hells Canyon.*** *Conservationists today released a plan for full protection of the spectacular Hells Canyon Country…as a constructive alternative to the series of controversial dams proposed by power companies. Joining Evans in support were Larry Williams, Oregon Vice President of the Federation of Western Outdoor Clubs; James Calvert, Moscow Idaho, Chair of the Inland Empire Group of the Sierra Club; and T. Russ Mager, Pocatello Idaho, President of the Hells Canyon Preservation Council…" "[T]he conservationists warned that a major battle over the fate of Hells Canyon is shaping up in Congress early next year…."*

Conservationists were gaining some momentum. According to Evans, another breakthrough came in summer 1969, when he went to Washington, DC, "to see if we could get the federal government to stop advocating more dams and come over to our side…."

His target was the incoming Nixon Administration, whose environmental credentials were unknown. Maybe there was a possibility here?

Evans remembered:

"… by chance a friend in Seattle learned I was traveling to DC, and she said 'you ought to look up my brother Buddy, who works at the White House!' Seizing that small straw of opportunity, I called up, and was soon ushered into the office of Bud Krogh. Learning that my mission was about dams and I was from the Northwest, Bud introduced me to John Erlichman, who I met some years earlier in Seattle. After assuring me that he was at heart a 'fanatic environmentalist,' he listened when I explained about the magnificence of Hells Canyon and the FPC hearings, and how important it would be for the new Republican government to get on our side instead of supporting that outmoded dam. Erlichman said 'wait a minute,' picked up his phone and got Russell Train, Undersecretary of the Interior, on the line. He explained who I was and what I wanted, then asked if I could be there at 2:30 today?"[28]

"Over I went, with my briefcase of photos and witness' testimony … and Train was very thoughtful and attentive. About a month later, the Department of the Interior stopped supporting the Appaloosa dam or any other dam."[29]

The courage to get out front was found in the newly-elected Senator Robert Packwood (R-OR), a liberal Republican. Boyd Norton, a wildlife photographer, took Evans's draft bill to Washington in 1969, along with some of his own photos. Stunned by the magnificent pictures, Packwood said:

6 Senator Robert Packwood (R-OR)

"I was raised all my life in Oregon, and I had no experience with the East till I went back to the Senate." The contrast was illuminating. "… [E]very month that I lived more in the East I made a little pledge to myself that what had happened to the East would not happen to Oregon."[30]

In response to the conservationists' proposal, Senator Packwood introduced the National River bill (S. 3329) in

January 1970 with 26 cosponsors from all parts of the political spectrum. Conservationists pleaded with Church to co-sponsor the bill. But he refused. Senator Mark Hatfield (R-OR), who sat on two the key committees, (the Committee on Appropriations and the Environment and Public Works Committee) refused to hold hearings on the bill.

Now the focus was national media. Boyd Norton reached out to Arthur Godfrey, host for many years of a popular weekday CBS radio variety show and later on television. In May 1970 Norton got Godfrey to fly to Lewiston, ride with Floyd Harvey, an Idaho boatman, down the river and spend the night at Harvey's ranch.

Harvey invited the Associated Press, United Press, and, of course, CBS. He would not let Idaho Republican Gov. Don Samuelson, a confirmed supporter of all the Idaho Power Company's dams, join the trip. Folk singer Burl Ives joined the party. The Lewiston Tribune reported:

"… Ives and Godfrey swapped yarns and traded Burl's guitar back and forth as they outdid each other with humorous backcountry ballads."[31]

The U.S. Forest Service provided horses for a trail ride up Sand Creek to give the party a feel for the canyon-face wilderness. The Department of the Interior supplied a helicopter, and Harvey had persuaded a floatplane pilot to land. The celebrities and the press saw it from every angle—and heard every environmental argument.[32]

In a letter to Interior Secretary Walter Hickel, Godfrey wrote:

"I would willingly attempt to swim the entire 96 or 7 miles up that

cold river from Lewiston just to see it again.... Mr. Secretary, I implore you, I beg of you: make the trip out there as soon as you possibly can and see this place for yourself. Better still; permit me to arrange a trip for you. I will personally fly you out there and introduce you to the warm, wonderful people who laid on the trip for me. ...I believe no one who has ever beheld its priceless, irreplaceable beauty would dream of building another dam there." [33]

Hickel agreed to a visit. In 1971, the Department announced that:

"It would henceforth 'at any time' oppose the building of High Mountain Sheep" and suggested that the Federal Power Commission "should give serious consideration to a recommendation that the middle Snake ... be brought under the provisions of the year-old National Wild and Scenic River System." [34]

Governor Samuelson arranged for a visit of a dam supporter Art Linkletter, another national radio and television host. He didn't get as far as Nez Perce, and those network cameramen got little footage. Harvey reported "it was a disaster. Linkletter's plane was delayed in Boise. The delay caused him to fail to see the Mountain Sheep site or much of the canyon." [35] In classic grassroots style, HCPC board member Anne Tussing arranged for her congressman, Mike McCormack (D-WA), then the only scientist in the House of Representatives, to raft the river in 1971. McCormack was so impressed with Hells Canyon, he brought two colleagues for a trip the following summer.

Still, there was no action on the national river bill in 1970. Packwood's senior colleague, the powerful Senator Mark Hatfield, was still opposed in 1971.

That same year, CBS organized a float trip with Senator Packwood that gave decisive new energy to his support for the National River concept.

> *"I remember the scene so well," said Evans, "all sitting around a campfire, listening to the roar of Granite Creek Rapids just waiting for us the next day ... and Packwood says 'Well, Brock, just what do you people really want here?' I asked if anyone had a map, and someone pulled out a highway map, upon which I drew the boundaries we had all agreed upon a year or so before. Back in Washington, Packwood had legislative counsel redraw the bill with the conservationist-agreed boundaries, which he then reintroduced in the Senate."*[36]

There was no House bill until 1970 when Representative John P. Saylor (R-PA), the senior Republican on the House Interior Committee, introduced a companion to Packwood's National River bill.

The House Interior Committee held a hearing on H.R. 15455 in September 1971. Governor Cecil Andrus (D-ID), represented governors Tom McCall (R-OR) and Dan Evans (R-WA) in a joint statement. Sitting in the front row waiting to testify, he was chatting with Doug Scott, who worked for the Wilderness Society, when a dam lobbyist on his other side leaned over to say to a colleague behind the governor:

> *"Can't you guys back in Idaho put the arm on that damned governor, he's killing us."*

Andrus nudged Doug and simply turned over the pile of his written statements, the large, gold embossed seal of the State of Idaho at the top. There was soon a sudden loud inhaling and the two observers left the room. It is one of Andrus's favorite stories.

Also in 1970, Representative Al Ullman (D-OR), whose district included Hells Canyon, finally changed his position in June 1970 by introducing the National Forest Parklands Area bill (HR 16437) of 750,000 acres.[37] Ullman's bill was cosponsored by Oregon Democrat Edith Green and Republican Wendell Wyatt. Williams, representing Oregon Environmental Council (OEC), found this draft bill wholly inadequate, surprising the Idaho group, which thought it an important step forward.

"There were many reasons for our opposition," Williams said, "It appeared the bill had been written by the Forest Service and did not reflect the environmentalists' idea of what such a bill should say."[38]

The bill prescribed no management guidelines except to say that the area would be managed under the Forest Service's Multiple Use Sustained Yield Act (P.L. 86-517, as amended), which allows for the "utilizing and disposal of natural resources." The bill would also have allowed continued leasing of mineral resources. The other danger was that Hatfield might be tempted to introduce Ullman's weak bill in the Senate—likely killing any chance that a stronger bill would survive (i.e.: as a rule, bills only get weaker as they work their way through the Congress). When next in Washington, Williams met with Ullman in his office. When he raised Hells Canyon, the congressman walked out on him.[39]

That year the FPC moratorium was before the Senate. When the legislation was on the Senate floor, Packwood considered adding his national rivers bill to it. He reluctantly decided against offering such an amendment. He reflected:

"The issue of Hells Canyon had been heard and heard, and studied and studied. It wasn't like you were springing something brand new on the floor of the Senate. I had tried to use Senate procedures and been rebuffed, so I thought – I'll go around 'em."[40]

However, in the end he reluctantly decided against taking such an action.

7 A day of drifting through quiet waters

A large delegation flew to Washington for a House hearing on the national river bill championed by Saylor. Godfrey testified briefly, calling the dams obscenities. The witnesses included Boyd Norton, Brock Evans, Pete Henault, Jim Campbell and Jerry Jayne from HCPC's Idaho chapter; Dale Storey of the Oregon Wallowa chapter of HCPC; John Barker, Lewiston Hells Canyon history expert; and Larry Williams, executive director of the newly formed OEC.

Long-time dam supporter Stewart Udall, the former Secretary of the Interior, endorsed the national river and admitted he'd been wrong about the environmental impact of dams. That was very significant, for he and his brother, powerful Representative Morris "Mo" Udall (D-AZ), would later oppose the dams proposed in the Grand Canyon—after Mo Udall left office in 1991.[41] The next day representatives of more than 40 organizations—from the Sierra Club to Bumble Bee Tuna—met and organized the Coalition to Save the

Snake. Momentum was growing. A new Idaho poll showed that 72 percent of the public supported the moratorium. [42]

8 Folk singer Jimmy Collier and Pete Seeger

Williams remembered that Dale Jones of Friends of the Earth arranged a float trip with Pete Seeger in July 1972 to help increase public support for saving the canyon.

Pete was America's river-saving troubadour. Also on the trip were folk singer Jimmy Collier, Mt. Everest climbers Willi Unsoeld and Lute Jerstad. On the trip, Seeger composed a song about the magnificent canyon using a tune called "Over the Waterfall:"

Seeger recorded the Hells Canyon song on his album "Banks of Marble." The song opens with his haunting yodel echoing off the high canyon walls. He then comes in with his unmatched five-string banjo picking. [43]

In 1972, Church finally changed his long-held pro-dam position, suggesting Hells Canyon should be a national recreation area. His newly elected colleague, Senator Jim McClure (R-ID), from Lewiston, joined him, although he had told HCPC secretary Dick Farman to "go back to Idaho and kick that [Pete] Henault in the kneecap."[44]

Slowly the political stage was being set for a new bill, reflecting a gathering consensus for better protection of the whole wilderness—the great river itself, plus its wild uplands.

In August 1973 Evans became director of the Sierra Club's Washington, DC office. His Seattle replacement was Doug Scott who had grown up in Portland and had been a lobbyist for The Wilderness Society and engaged in the Hells Canyon effort, working with Senators Packwood and Church. The basic idea was that there would be no dams. The three governors and the key legislators of both parties agreed. So, working from the best ideas in previous bills, drafts, strategy memos, and correspondence as well as clear precedents, HCPC President Henault and Scott and key congressional staff drafted a straightforward bill. It provided for no dams, wild and scenic river status for the main canyon and a portion of the Rapid River tributary, and wilderness for the canyon walls and slopes on both sides.

MOVING HATFIELD

Meanwhile, the four senators (Hatfield, Packwood, Church and McClure) from the affected states conducted talks through summer 1973. Ullman, though frustrated by Williams's hard line response to his bill, was generally moving toward supporting the legislation. Hatfield was not. He was furious about the growing public pressure and particularly the public criticism Williams and others had unleashed in the Oregon newspapers and television news. "Why to get into politics if you can't take criticism?" mused Williams on hearing that news.

"In 1973 I called Hatfield's senior aide, Gerry Frank," Williams recalled, "because we were frustrated with Hatfield's refusal to support Packwood's Hells Canyon bill. I questioned Gerry as to why the senator was refusing to support Packwood's legislation. He told me that he was good friends with Congressman George Hansen (R-ID) who, though not from the district involved, was a strong supporter of building a dam. Frank saw that the relationship made it impossible for Hatfield to support saving Hells Canyon.

"With that news I drafted a press release saying that Hatfield was opposed to saving Hells Canyon. I faxed an advance copy to Hatfield's office in Washington as a courtesy and then distributed it to the press. I soon got a very angry call from another Hatfield

aide, Walt Evans, asking how I dared to make up such an outrageous statement. 'Who told you that Hatfield was against saving Hells Canyon,' he asked. I told him I had spoken to Gerry Frank who confirmed Hatfield's opposition to saving the canyon."[45]

"That kind of focused pressure does work when our preferred course of friendly persuasion fails," Williams observed. "Within the next few days Hatfield switched sides and signed onto the Packwood bill. That was after the senator called the OEC office and thoroughly chewed out my administrative assistant, Judie Hansen. She was still shaking when I returned to the office."[46]

With Hatfield on board, staff members for Church, McClure, Packwood, and Hatfield worked out boundaries and the senators met to finalize language. Church introduced the "four senators' bill," S. 2233, in summer 1973. The language was carefully calibrated to cover Ullman's concerns. At last there was consensus on a vastly improved national recreation area bill.   The Senate Interior Committee held field hearings in La Grande, Oregon and Lewiston, Idaho on December 6, 14, and 15, 1973.[47] A House Interior subcommittee held a Washington, DC hearing on April 23, 1974, soon after the opening of the second session of the 94th Congress. Conservationists expected that the Forest Service would support the bill. Learning of the Forest Service's new non-position, Scott sent a confidential memo to conservation leaders.

"On the basis of soundings in recent weeks, our expectation had been that the Forest Service would come in with a reasonable position … Surprise! They got unplugged. The Deputy Chief showed up to say they had no position at all. The agency was preparing its own alternative position: whereupon the whole thing was adjourned for 60 days."[48]

9 Pete Seeger on the banjo with Willi Unsold, the first person to climb the west ridge of Mt. Everest, on the harmonica

When the subcommittee met to vote in November 1974, the key question was whether there would be a quorum of supporters to allow a committee vote? As a result of a scandal involving his predecessor, Al Ullman was now acting chairman of the powerful Ways and Means Committee; he could put extraordinary pressure on any wavering Democrat. However, he was elsewhere that morning. Evans and Scott worked with Ullman's staff to find him to call absent Democrats, and then go to the meeting room to personally buttonhole his colleagues for their support of the bill. Ullman arrived, and, as members entered, Ullman planted himself where they had to walk close to him so his presence could help to get the needed votes.

On December 11, 1974, the full House Interior Committee approved the bill 22 to 7, sending it to the floor. But there was no time on the House calendar for a vote before the Thanksgiving recess. This delay could have easily killed the bill. The second session of the 94th Congress ended without further progress[49]

"The next year," Scott recalled, "… in January, in the very first days of the first session of the 95th Congress, we secured the co-sponsorship of the so called "Ullman bill" by almost a majority of the Senate Interior Committee. The Senate passed the "four senators bill" on June 2, 1975, shifting the spotlight to the House.[50]

Rattled, the power interests saw they could not stop the bill but would have to try to gut it by amendment. And thus, almost out of desperation was born the dam builder's last weapon—a device so brilliantly conceived and carefully executed that the sheer genius of it continues to be admired, even by its enemies. With a few minor changes—a few words here, a few words there—the bill could be altered so that the prohibition against dams applied *only to the downstream half of the canyon.* The wilderness would stay the same, as the wilderness boundary did not touch the river itself.

Representative Teno Roncalio (D-WY) with Oregon's Bob Duncan (D-OR), proposed the power interest's amendments. On the committee, the new champion for the conservationists was a feisty congressman from north of Seattle, Lloyd Meeds (D-WA). As a senior member of the Interior Committee his office became the nerve center for the conservation lobbyists.

Scott remembered that the key media tag line was that Hells Canyon was "the deepest gorge in North America." In a laughable moment in the lobbying, Meeds called Scott to say he'd received a fancy packet of materials from the Idaho Power Company. (Scott observed that it isn't particularly smart to give your materials to the leader for your opponents.)

"I ran over and leafed through their propaganda," he remembers. "To show the location of the canyon, they had included a folded National Geographic Society map … which featured a red arrow pointing out Hells Canyon and labeled 'Deepest Gorge in North America.'[51] In addition, a rendering of the river after the dam was in place showed the river looking just the same as it is without the dam — no reservoir!"[52]

They undermined their own pitch that there is nothing of value at the proposed dam site.

Pro-river forces won handily on November 18, 1975 as the House Interior Committee approved the bill, one much like the bill already passed by the Senate. The next stop was the Rules Committee and then onto the House floor under a procedural rule to set the terms of the debate and vote.

THE END GAME

Scott was in Seattle the morning the bill would go to the Rules Committee. Help was needed to make all the necessary phone calls. At 10:30 a.m. Meeds called to say they had just received the rule that the bill would be debated and open for amendment for one hour later that day.[53]

Evans, Jones, and Scott went wild, making call after call to the offices of supportive House members, for only they and Meeds and a couple of others knew the bill would be up for a vote shortly. Ullman was busy with a tax bill expected to come to the floor next; he didn't know the change, nor did his staffer Bill Alsburger when Scott reached him. Scott's Sierra Club colleague Chuck Clusen, in the Washington, DC office, dropped everything to line up others. They began calling every friendly House office, talking to staffers to turn out the troops for Meeds and Ullman.

Fronting for the dam coalition, Representative Keith Sebelius (R-KA), a dam proponent, began to argue for yet another moratorium, a desperate attempt to block the conservation bill. Meeds lost his temper:

"There was a moratorium proposed in the Senate. The Senate has twice repudiated that moratorium by the passage of the legislation before us, so there is no moratorium. We have run out of

moratoriums. We have run out of time. It is time now to make up our minds about preserving this area."[54]

Given his seniority, Chairman Ullman had the last word. He spoke eloquently:

"The highest and best use of this vast and spectacularly beautiful area is to allow this free-flowing river to remain in its present state in this tremendous canyon. That is what this bill does." He continued, *"The area has been studied to death. We are now at the point of decision, and it is time to make a final disposition of this area and adopt this bill."*[55]

The few differences in the two versions were quickly resolved and on November 12 and 18, 1975 respectively, the Senate and House passed the Hells Canyon bill.

In a titanic struggle between a rising force in American politics—the environmental movement—and a fading force, the dam builders—the environmentalists won. In the process, they overturned political assumptions of both parties in the Northwest and allied themselves with courageous senators and representatives who stepped up to help move their more unenlightened, pro-dam colleagues. The honor roll includes Senators Packwood and Church, Representatives Ullman and Meeds, and Governors Tom McCall (Oregon), Daniel Evans (Washington), and Cecil Andrus (Idaho).

On the last day of 1975, President Gerald Ford signed Public Law 94-199, "An Act to Establish the Hells Canyon National Recreation Area in the States of Oregon and Idaho, and for Other Purposes."[56] The 218,018-acre Hells Canyon Wilderness Area enjoyed the full statutory protection of the 1964 Wilderness Act—134,208 acres on the Idaho side, and 83,811 acres on the Oregon flank.[57] A 71-mile stretch of the Middle Snake through the canyon was designated a wild river, along with 27 miles of the tributary Rapid River, on the Idaho side. And, icing on the cake, Section 6(a) provided:

"Notwithstanding any other provision of law, or any authorization heretofore given pursuant to law, the Federal Power Commission may not license the construction of any dam, water conduit, reservoir, powerhouse, transmission line or power work...."

10 Oregon Governor Bob Straub at the podium

In a final flourish, the bill included a provision specifically forbidding one more dam, *outside* the NRA boundary: Asotin Dam, near Lewiston, slated to be a reregulating dam for those upstream.

"I don't think there ever has been another statute which specifically forbids a proposed dam by name," says Brock Evans.

On July 31, 1976, the Forest Service held a dedication of the Hells Canyon National Recreation Area at Hat Point, overlooking the deep and wild canyon. Though grassroots and national environmental leaders were not invited to take part in the ceremony, they were not completely forgotten on that day.

11 Representative Al Ullman (R-OR) and Senator Robert Packwood (R-OR) unveiling the commemorative plaque. (The plaque was subsequently lost during a Forest Service renovation of Hat Point.)

The Forest Service placed a large brass plaque at the overlook reading:

This site marked in tribute to those that had the perception and foresight, and willingly made sacrifices to preserve forever the untamed reaches of Hells Canyon of the Snake River along with the wild and scenic beauty of this area. This area designated by Congress and signed into law by the President of the United States on December 31, 1975.

This plaque is placed in honor of the American people and in dedication to Hells Canyon National Recreation Area.

EPILOUGE

Hells Canyon was saved. The river shall flow, forever wild and undammed. The wild canyon walls, home to mountain sheep and deer, will remain wild, raptors soaring high above. The river, the sheep, the deer, and the ghosts of so many explorers, miners, homesteaders, hunters, trappers, and conservationists are looking on, surely with great approval of a job well done.

The dedication day did confirm an unintended fact: the new Hells Canyon National Recreation Area represented, above all else, a huge shift in energy policy and nothing less than a transformation of environmental politics in Oregon and the rest of the Northwest.

A small group of conservation staff leaders augmented the work of dedicated grassroots volunteers. These leaders were young people with deep knowledge of the strategies and tactics by which the media can help and by which public laws are made.

THE AUTHORS

Larry Williams served as the Oregon Vice President for the Federation of Western Outdoor Clubs and then Chair of the North West Chapter of the Sierra Club. He then became the executive director of the Oregon Environmental Council during the period covered here, and later served on the staff of the White House Council on Environmental Quality during the administration of President Jimmy Carter, and later became the director of the Sierra Club's international program. In 2008 he received the Lifetime Achievement Award from the Oregon Environmental Council. He co-authored a book, *International Banks and the Environment.* He lives in Washington, DC. lwindc@starpower.net.

Brock Evans, an attorney by training, led the filings in the vital Federal Power Commission licensing proceedings that achieved delay when most needed. He was the Sierra Club's Northwest Representative during the struggle against the Snake River dams. Later, he was the Sierra Club's chief lobbyist in Washington, DC during final passage of the Hells Canyon National Recreation Act bill. He is also the author of a recent prize-winning book, *Fight and Win* about successful environmental campaigns. In 1981 he also received the Sierra Club's highest honor, the John Muir Award. He lives in La Grande, OR. brockevans2004@gmail.com

Doug Scott, a forester by training, coordinated the largest Earth Day program at that time on the campus of the University of Michigan and served on the board of directors of the national coordinating nonprofit for the original Earth Day 1970. He was a lobbyist for The Wilderness Society in Washington, DC, and then became Northwest Representative for the Sierra Club during the years covered here. He later was chief Sierra Club lobbyist for the Alaska National Interest Lands Conservation Act of 1980 and 1997 received the Sierra Club's highest honor, the John Muir Award. He is the author of three books and many magazine articles and principal of Doug Scott Wilderness Consulting. He lives in Palm Springs, CA. scottdoug959@gmail.com.

END NOTES

Note to readers: The website www.congress.gov provides information (bill numbers, hearing dates, actions, votes, etc.) about bills cited below for dates in 1973 or later. However, for older bills, less information (such as bill or law texts) is provided. Information on bill or law texts can be obtained in federal deposit libraries or through commercial legal data bases; the latter generally charge fees.

---

[1] 16 U.S.C § 460gg (2000), P. L. No. 94-199.

[2] William O. Douglas, *Of Men and Mountains* (New York: Harper & Brothers Publishers, 1950), p. 236.

[3] fs.usda.gov/detail/wallowa-whitman/specialplaces.Viewed on April 20, 2018.

[4] Richard L. Neuberger. *Our Promised Land.* New York, NY. The Macmillan Company. 1938, pp. 354-355.

[5] Ibid, p. 97.

[6] The Oregon Historical Society offers details and photographs of the flood.

[7] Karl Brooks, Public Power, Private Dams, The Hells Canyon High Dam Controversy, University of Washington Press, 2006. p. 61.

[8] Ibid: p. 176.

[9] Brock Evans, personal recollection.

[10] Udall v. Federal Power Commission, 387 U.S. 428 (1967) 387 U.S. 428.

[11] Ibid.

[12] Letter of June 30, 1967 to the Federal Power Commission for intervention in the Project No. 2243 and 2273, the High Mountain Sheep Project, from Brock Evans.

[14] Ibid.

[14] "Petition of Intervention, filed August 31, 1967, Brock Evans, Sierra Club Northwest Office Papers, University of Washington Special Collections.

[15] William Ashworth, Hells Canyon: the Deepest Gorge on Earth (New York: Hawthorn Books, 1977), p. 5. (Hereafter referred to as "Ashworth.")

[16] Evans, Hells Canyon internal campaign memo, December 29, 1972.

[17] Hells Canyon Story (1967-68*)*, Brock Evans' draft article for *The Falcon*, HCPC Newsletter, (2000), Document #1, personal files.

[18] Ibid.

[19] Levy decision issued early 1971: Brock Evans, Hells Canyon campaign internal campaign memo, Dec. 29, 1972.

[20] Ashworth, p. 151.

22 Gerald Williams, *The U.S. Forest Service in the Pacific Northwest – A History,* (Corvallis, Oregon State University Press, 2009), p. 242.

22 Now called the Greater Hells Canyon Council. The name was changed in 2017 to reflect an expanded mission. Since this is a book about how Hells Canyon and its immediate environs were saved, this book will continue reference to the predecessor organization that existed at the time. The eight founders of the Council were: Boyd Norton, Jerry Jayne, Al McGlinsky, Russ Mager, Cyril Slansky, Jim Campbell, Jack Bary and Paul Fritz.

23 Ashworth, p. 148.

24 Ibid

25 Brock Evans internal memos, Hells Canyon Campaign, December 1972-January 1973.

26 Sara Dant, "Making Wilderness Work: Frank Church and the American Wilderness Movement," *Pacific Historical Review* Vol. 77. No. 2 (May 2008), pp. 237-272.

27 Frank Church to Dear Friend, October 1969, file 22, box 3, MS 124, Hutchinson Papers Boise State University.

28 Brock Evans, internal Hells Canyon campaign memo, January 1973.

29 Ibid

30 Ashworth, p. 159.

31 Lewiston Tribune, "Preservation of the Wild Waters of the Snake," January 19, 1994.

32 Ashworth, p. 164.

33 Ibid, p. 162.

34 Ibid, p. 156.

35 Ibid, p. 164.

36 Brock Evans, personal communication, January 21, 2015.

37 Ashworth, pp. 181-182.

38 Letter from the Oregon Environmental Council to Al Ullman, *Earthwatch Oregon,* March, 8, 1973.

39 Larry Williams, oral history, with Oregon Historical Society, April 8-9, 2008.

40 Ashworth, p. 169.

41 Doug Scott, personal recollection, January 18, 2015.

42 "Knowing there would be wonderful music around the campfire, I brought along a cassette recorder and my camera," Williams recalled. "I was not disappointed. I recorded singing during all those sun and water-filled days in the wilderness. Along with Pete's banjo we had Jimmy's guitar, Willi's harmonica, and a flute player. Pete wrote a song to the tune of 'Over the Waterfall,' calling on the politicians to save Hells Canyon. A few weeks later I got a card from Pete asking me to share with him the recording of his Hells Canyon song for he had forgotten the words. I sent him a tape of the song; it became the lead piece on his new album 'Banks of Marble.'" Folkways Records, Smithsonian Institution, 1972. Larry Williams, personal recollection.

43 A video of Pete Seeger and the rafters, opening with his yodels echoing from the canyon walls when he sings, with his banjo, the song he wrote to help in the campaign to protect Hells Canyon, is at larry-williams.magix.net.

44 Pete Henault was president of the Hells Canyon Preservation Council from 1970 to 1972.

---

[45] Larry Williams, oral history, Oregon Historical Society, April 8-9, 2008.
[46] Ibid.
[47] Ashworth, p. 188. Hearings before Subcommittee on Parks and Recreation of Senate Interior & Insular Affairs on S. 657 and S. 2233, December 6, 14 & 15 1973.
[48] Ibid, p. 190.
[49] Ibid, pp. 190-195.
[50] S. 322. The text of older bills is not available from the congressional website.
[51] National Geographic, undated map.
[52] Larry Williams, oral history, with Oregon Historical Society, April 8-9, 2008.
[53] Ashworth, pp. 201-203.
[54] Ibid, p. 209.
[55] Ibid, pp. 209-210.
[56] Public Law 94-199, December 31, 1975.
[57] Definitive acreages, a general boundary map, and the text of the law are at http://www.wilderness.net/NWPS/wildView?WID=239, a site maintained by the U.S. Forest Service, the other three federal wilderness agencies, and the University of Montana.

www.ingramcontent.com/pod-product-compliance
Lightning Source LLC
Chambersburg PA
CBHW040240240726
48664CB00001B/215